The Secret Life of the
MOUNTAIN HARE

The Secret Life of the
MOUNTAIN HARE

Andy Howard

Foreword: Iolo Williams

First published in Great Britain in 2018
Sandstone Press Ltd
Dochcarty Road
Dingwall
Ross-shire
IV15 9UG
Scotland

This edition 2020

www.sandstonepress.com

The publisher acknowledges subsidy from Creative Scotland towards publication of this volume.

ISBN: 978-1-913207-26-7

Jacket and book design by Raspberry Creative Type, Edinburgh
Printed and bound in China by Imago

Acknowledgements

I'd like to thank my dear parents for nurturing my love of nature and the great outdoors from my early beginnings. Bill and Terry Fraser for giving me the faith to go-it-alone; you were right! To Douglas Willis and Betty Morris, two of my former school teachers, for the encouragement and the difficult task of engaging a young and wondering mind. Robert Davidson and the team at Sandstone Press for having faith in this project.

There are so many individuals that are worthy of mention that have given me support. Here are a few that have offered me a helping hand in one way or another, I thank them all: Iolo Williams, Chris Sharrat, Derek McGinn, Charlie Philips, Pete Walkden, Kate MacRae, Mark Hamblin, Pete Cairns, Neil McIntyre, Andrew Simpson, Kenny and the boys, the team at Ffordes Photographic, Sam and the girls at Keela, the team at Tweed Media, and Leica.

To my darling wife Lyndsey, who is far too wise for her years.
Lyndsey thank you for your unending love and support.

Contents

Foreword

There is nothing I like more than spending a day in the field with a person who really knows his or her subject. It is an unadulterated joy to walk the British countryside in such company, teasing out information whilst watching the wildlife in question. One such individual is Andy Howard, particularly when the subject is mountain hares. An encyclopaedia of knowledge, a walking, talking lagomorph google, he truly understands the full meaning of each twitch of a mountain hare's nose and every flick of its ear, but that is far from all that he is.

Andy is also a stunning wildlife photographer, a man at the very peak of his profession. This book takes us from his initial encounters with this enigmatic species through to many of his most recent. Such has been his dedication and devotion that Andy has got to know many of the hares as individuals, identifying the subtle differences in behaviour that make them such interesting subjects.

Lavishly illustrated with many of his beautiful photographs, *The Secret Life of the Mountain Hare* is a wonderful mix of personal encounters intertwined with the science of mountain hare ecology through the four seasons. Without doubt, the mountain hare is a stunning and fascinating creature. However, it is also under threat from misguided moorland managers in some parts of Scotland. This book will undoubtedly help to build a wider public appreciation of a species that is incredibly well adapted to the most hostile of British environments.

If you have not seen a mountain hare galloping with consummate ease over rough mountain terrain or sitting tight amongst clumps of heather in a snowstorm, I urge you to visit the high expanses of the Highlands of Scotland or the north of England as soon as you possibly can. Alternatively, you can buy Andy's book and gaze longingly over each page as if you were accompanying the man himself on the mountains.

Iolo Williams
Mid-Wales
April 2018

INTRODUCTION

Having drawn into the first layby south of Slochd summit, on the A9, I took a rucksack, camera and other photographic gear and ascended the hill to the east, intent on my first picture of a mountain hare. The going was steep, the ground rough underfoot, and my load was heavy, but that was not new. I had been photographing wildlife since my wife, Lyndsey, and I decided that my earlier passion of salmon fishing was too mutually exclusive. This we could share.

Our lives had been altered at, of all things, a dinner party when one of our guests suggested that, to be world class at anything, it is necessary to specialise. I decided that my focus for five years would be five species: dotterel, red grouse, crested tit, ptarmigan and mountain hare, the only mammal. Of these I had so far photographed all four birds, but no mountain hares.

At that time, indeed until recently, they had not been photographed extensively. Other than experts, few people knew all that much about them, or much cared. In the few years that have passed since that morning above Slochd, public awareness has increased beyond belief and these amazing animals have begun to be appreciated for what they are and the magic they bring to the landscape. This turnaround, I believe, has been substantially achieved by the photographers who first specialised in capturing their images.

Casting around for where I might locate such a thing as a mountain hare, I received several suggestions and was heading for a hill behind Kingussie, in Strathspey, when I spotted two dead animals by the side of the road. This was clue enough to set me on my fateful journey, not to the top of the hill but to an area of elevated peatland where, ahead of me, nestled into a soft ledge within a peat hag, I spotted what at first looked like a length of bleached bogwood. Maybe it was something else. I fitted a suitable lens to my

Posing for the camera.

camera and zoomed into, yes, the face of a mountain hare: its distinctive eyes and ears.

Now I had my first picture I felt relaxed, somewhat justified, in my quest. In the course of the afternoon I had several fascinating encounters with mountain hares and this word 'encounter' became part of my expedition lexicon. Each was different not only because of location, light, and weather, but also because each hare is an individual. To look in its eyes is to search and, sometimes, be searched. Over the following years certain individuals would find their places in my heart.

Soon, the odd picture of mine began to appear in magazines, and eventually on the BBC nature programme *Springwatch*. Illustrating an article on 'The Masters of Disguise' by Patrick Laurie some appeared in, of all possible outlets, the *Shooting Gazette*. The irony did not go past me, but my own, reluctant moral compromise proved justified by an email from a reader who said that, persuaded by my photographs, he would not kill mountain hares again. I was on the road to professionalism.

My article on 'How to Photograph Mountain Hares' on the website *Nature TTL* completed the job and soon I had set up as a guide and tutor visiting three locations frequently. One is in the Northern Corries of the Cairngorms, two others are in the Monadhliath mountains. Very different landscapes, divided by the A9, the Cairngorms and the Monadhliath together make up

Haloed by golden light.

probably the most varied, most vast area of wild land in Britain. From my viewpoint above Slochd I could make out both but had no idea of their significance in my future life.

There was no guidebook to follow, no mentor to emulate. I had no idea how to approach them, no idea of their intelligence, of their charm beyond the superficial. I did not understand that, with patience on my part, they would get used to me and come to accept the presence of this particular human and his camera. It took two years. By then though, I had a good idea of their body language and behavior. Mountain hares make very few sounds. Instead they roll on the ground and urinate to leave their scent. Among their primary messages are the sexual preparedness of the jill. Is she in season or out?

They are placid in the extreme, wandering outside their inherited territories rarely if at all. Violence is virtually unknown except prior to mating when they indulge their most famous anthropomorphic feature, known as 'boxing'. This is done between males and females, when the jack will make his approach only to be rebuffed. He may believe she is ready when, in fact, she is still not quite in season. He sidles behind her, sniffs interestedly, and before he knows it she has spun on those powerful hind legs and knocked him flying. In an instant both are upright, jabbing away, until they either mate or he runs off, usually in the direction from whence he came. In this way the jill might test the strength of several suitors as she comes into season and makes her choice. The wise jack will wait, not spending his strength in idle play. The special hare I named Bagpuss was adept at this, a master of timing.

Placid, yes, but they can defend themselves and their offspring in times of need and predators are aware of this. Their front paws are fitted with hard, extremely sharp, non-retractable claws and I have seen a hungry stoat, surely among the most savage and determined of hunters, give them a wide berth on his road to the easier prey that is rabbit. I have also seen a raven chased by a jill leaping into the air and swiping with her claws.

Rabbits (*Oryctolagus cuniculus*) are cousins to hares within the order *Lagomorpha*, and the johnny-come-latelies of the group, introduced after the Norman Conquest. Of hares the British Isles have three types: the brown hare (*Lepus europaeus*) arrived with the Romans, possibly the Anglo-saxons, the Irish hare (*Lepus timidus hibernicus*) is a much more recent import, introduced for sporting purposes and mostly found on the Isle of Mull (sometimes known as 'the officers' mess'), and the mountain hare (*Lepus timidus*) which goes back 10,000 years to the last major ice age. The mountain hare is mostly Scottish, but small populations survive in places they were located for sporting purposes.

In time I became more knowledgeable and increasingly committed. Magazine and web success led to television appearances and consultancy work on BBC's *The One Show* and *Countryfile* until, in June 2015, Lyndsey and I took our life's great risk. I went full time with her moral and financial support and, since then, have created an extensive photographic library and contributed articles and columns.

Moorland has become my second home because mountain hares live on the high pastures that were formerly used for cattle, and the rougher grazing that lies beside them. By choice they would live in forests but, in terms of habitat, they share the fate of the red deer. Evolved for forest living they

The author with the BBC Countryfile
presenter Ellie Harrison.

find themselves in territory denuded of trees. They have adapted to these conditions though, and thrive particularly on managed grouse moors, making them a principal subject in one of the great confrontations of our time: the head on collision of modern conservation requirements and traditional management methods.

To increase the numbers of grouse, and therefore the sporting value of the estate, owners and gamekeepers manage the predator species that take the grouse, but also take mountain hares. The hares have some sporting value for overseas shooters but, nonetheless, increasing hare numbers results in… too many hares for estate purposes. As is obvious, the balance that uninterrupted nature would create is thrown out of kilter and the chosen answer is the gun. There is no legal restriction on the numbers that may be killed during the hare culling season.

Although Scottish Natural Heritage has asked for 'restraint', little is demonstrated, and mass culls are organised frequently with horrific pictures bearing witness to the slaughter. In addition to the cruelty inflicted on this lovely, sentient creature, there is created an unnatural fragmentation of the population. Since they will not travel all that far from their point of origin they become island nations subject to inbreeding and further deprivation. This is a heart rending and surely unnecessary state of affairs that, rightly, brings further scrutiny to the shooting estates in addition to that inspired by raptor persecution, moor burning, and recreational access.

Often, I ask why the hares chose me, because that is how it feels. Take recreation, such as I offer to my clients, as *re*-creation and that is the effect these encounters have on tired, city-bound humanity. To watch them at close range is to enter a timeless peace. Over and again my clients report feelings of humility and emotional wellbeing. Close observation brings its own rewards as the animals reveal themselves unknowingly.

Unlike rabbits they do not live in holes in the ground, although they may use burrows as bolt holes. Instead they find undulations in the landscape where they can turn and make a shape in the heather, or peat hags, or boulders, or lengths of ancient bogwood to shelter behind. These locations are called 'forms' and some have been used by generations of hares. Their lives mostly consist of drowsing in apparent idleness before they display their chewing, whisker-twitching signs of coming wakefulness. Then they will wander, grazing, but ever prepared for those massive hind legs to take powerful flight. Seasonally, they will have romance on their minds.

They will appear to be unobservant, but this is deceiving. Once I noticed a hare was displaying what I had come to recognise as signs of distress. Could it be our presence? I thought not as we had followed the usual routines and the hare was familiar with me. Looking behind us, peering into the light for quite a while, I eventually spotted a distant raven, little more than a shape in the sky. Not a bird that presents a threat, it would look enough like an eagle to put the hare into a state of troubled alert. The sky demands a lot of hare attention for that reason, and it seems they have grown used to the planes coming into Inverness Airport as they can be seen following them with their eyes.

I find them to be captivating, mysterious, and rather fey. With 10,000 years of shared history, their human significance rests in the pagan religions that form our deep, pre-Christian mythology. After so long, culturally, they are as much *of* us as *with* us. Their faces are sources of fascination. To look in their eyes, as we do with our telephoto lenses, is to view a deep black pupil with a sort of burnt orange iris, surrounded by fine eyelashes. The burnt orange, I should say, alters with the years and gives a clue to the animal's age.

Their pelage morphs three times a year: from white to brown in spring, brown to grey in autumn, and a return to white for the next winter. Their whiskers may be black or white, an observation I have not noted from any source other than my own viewing. In my experience, they live from four to five years.

Their ears are relatively short, and black tipped, and have four main positions: upright and alert, flat back which displays anxiety, even fear, certainly deep distress, or tucked in to prevent heat loss while they rest. The male's ears point forward when it is in a post-coital condition. Returning to that first picture, taken above the Slochd, I recognise my hare's distress and this I regret. My approach was clumsy but I still had so much to learn as, indeed, I still do.

The literature of the mountain hare is mostly academic, rarely observational or emotional. This book may go some way to rectifying that. Our days on the hill, my clients' and mine, go with the sun. How long will we stay here, I might be asked at the beginning of an encounter, and I will point to a hill and say, 'until the sun touches that slope'.

LEFT: My first experience with a mountain hare, this one was alarmed by my presence.

ABOVE: The perfect form, temporarily vacated.

LEFT: First cousins, the brown hare...
ABOVE: ...and the Irish hare.

HABITAT

The main strongholds of the mountain hare in Britain are the Grampians and the Southern Uplands of Scotland. The Grampians are not a single mountain range but the vast area between the Great Glen and the Highland Boundary Fault, which includes several mountain areas. The human population is of low density and settlements are relatively far apart, and it mostly consists of what is these days known as 'wild land'. Other mountain hare areas include the Peak District in Derbyshire and the Isle of Man, where they have been introduced, from Scotland, for sporting purposes. Other, smaller, mountain hare populations exist in Shetland, the Isle of Lewis, and Hoy (Orkney). Favoured terrains include: mountains, heath and moorland, flood plains, especially in the higher reaches of the watershed, rolling hills and grouse moors.

Of these, the high mountains are by far the most demanding, areas such as the Northern Corries of the Cairngorms, where I photograph often: high and bleak, cliff-girt and rocky, thinly vegetated. For the botanist the pickings are rich if sparse: plants such as bearberry and cloudberry, tormentil and isolated tufts of heather very different from those in the glens. Alpine flowers that have survived up here since the last major ice age include rare species like alpine saxifrage and hare's-foot sedge. Here, only specialist plants and animals can survive. The mountain hare is one, another is the ptarmigan, and the finding of food and shelter are their main priorities along with the conservation of energy.

On this terrain the hares know from which quarter the prevailing wind blows and make their silent, solitary stances on the steepest lee side. Should the wind change, and take on any great severity, the entire population migrates to a more sheltered quarter, returning later not only to the more familiar slope but also to the very spot they earlier vacated: their own private form.

Moor, trees and hill.

Anything that will serve as protection from the elements can be utilised. Any ditch, any rock, any undulation in the topography will do, and I have seen them take semi-permanent shelter behind ski fences and associated buildings. Peat hags are much favoured but more to be found among heath and moorland at much lower levels, the same biomass that receives so much attention as our planet's largest depository of carbon dioxide.

A bane to recreational hillwalkers on their way to a Munro or Corbett, the hags are deep gashes created by water erosion. Sometimes they begin when fire strips the surface of its protective heather, and they are often exacerbated by the passage of wildlife such as deer, who will wallow in the wet peat to keep cool and to armour themselves against insect attack. The weather does the rest.

Generations of hares have made their forms here, and some of the forms are used by generations of hares. They dig into the steep soft sides and settle against the wind. They make their tracks across the surface: faint lines walkers might pass without much noticing. The forms and paths may go back for centuries for all we can tell. Why not? When flooding forces them from the hags they will take what shelter they can behind a grassy tussock, eventually returning to the familiar and safe.

Sometimes though, they will descend to the flood plains of rivers such as the Spey and Findhorn in their

higher reaches and tributaries, but a few choose to remain, resting under the overhanging banks that have been carved by rushing water, especially at bends. They will even make their homes among the boulders. More hospitable are the lower reaches of the less craggy, rolling hills where they will inhabit natural terraces on the slopes, especially making their homes among juniper bushes. On the same terrain there are likely to be unfenced forests and small copses of trees such as birch and willow, but sometimes this can put them wrong with forest managers who do not like them nibbling at the bark. Too often for the hares, this can lead to 'managing' of the wrong type, with the gun.

Interaction with man is impossible to avoid and is not always to the good. When we have heavy weather in the highlands the Roads Department deploys its ploughs and great banks of snow are piled at the road edges. Hares have no road sense, and often leap down on a surface that is easier to walk on. They can't leap back, unfortunately, and I once counted forty dead on my way home before stopping counting.

A still greater place of conflict is the grouse moor, where drainage ditches are much favoured and, irony of ironies, shooting butts. Of all land in Scotland, the grouse moors are the most heavily managed, on some to the point of monoculture, but only the most recent generation of owners and gamekeepers has considered such a condition to be desirable. Since it runs against their own traditions as well as being an affront to nature, the only possible question is: *Why?*

The absence of predators makes this an even more attractive environment for the hares, and with no other grazing animals the eating is good. Their presence, of course, acts as a call back to the raptors: eagles, buzzards and hawks, and the temptation for the estates to enter a cycle of slaughter is not often enough resisted.

LEFT: The perfect mixed habitat.

ABOVE: Settling with her back to the wind.

Field Note

Admiring the view

Fuelled with enthusiasm after a successful early morning visit to a black grouse lek, I paid a visit to my favourite mountain hare location in the Monadhliath. Conditions were good, the light was spot on, and I was bounding uphill when I spotted a hare doing much the same thing close by.

Intent on the vista as much as the animal, I was rather overwhelmed by the drama of the scene. Carefully positioning it to be small in the frame the result was this 'room with a view' image that, successfully I think, places the subject in the context of its landscape.

LEFT: Ideal hare country.

ABOVE: Man marks the landscape.
NB These are guides, not shooters.

ABOVE: Muir burning.

RIGHT: Sheltering in a peat hag.

Field Note

Off piste hare

Scanning the area around Coire Cas with my binoculars I spotted this hare taking refuge from a biting wind by the back door of the Scottish Ski Club hut. This caused my two clients great amusement. Had it paid its membership, or was it more like the Club cat waiting at the door to be taken in?

Actually, we were doing much the same by sheltering behind the walls of the old, now disused, Shieling Restaurant.

PREDATORS

Scotland's undoubted monarch of all predators, the darkest shadow on the mountain hare's world, is one of the world's largest birds, the golden eagle. The mature bird's wingspan may extend to more than two metres and its overall length to over a metre. Its beak is one of the most effective piercing and tearing tools in nature and the iron-hard, claw part of its talons may be more than five centimetres in length. They usually mate for life with the female being the larger of the pair, as with most raptors, and will raise two or three chicks at a time. They like to eat mountain hares.

My first close encounter with one of these apex predators was on the moorlands east of Tomatin when I was lost in concentration before a sitting hare. Suddenly, I noticed a distinct change in its demeanour. Its eyes became dilated and it cowered, trembling, back into its form, exhibiting the sort of behaviour I would expect in a human under extreme duress. At first, I thought I had done something wrong, that I had inadvertently frightened the poor creature, but some instinct made me look up and behind, to where an eagle was hanging on the wind, gliding silently over the moorland.

It was quartering the ground in a methodical manner, hugging it low while scanning the heather and the peat hags, hoping to spook out prey. As I watched, it stooped to ground, attempting a hit, unsuccessful this time, on a running hare. This one was on its own, but they also hunt in pairs, and how intelligent they are in their methods is obvious to any observer.

One of my birdwatching friends in the Monadhliath told me how he once spotted an eagle hovering on the wind above a juniper bush. Through his binoculars he saw, first, a terrified hare under the bush's canopy and, second, another eagle on the ground, advancing clumsily towards the bush although it could not possibly make its way inside. The hare was spooked. It ran, and

Golden Eagle and Raven.

its life was ended in a moment. When cloud cover is low, they will rise and fall in their flight, coming in and out of sight so as not to alarm potential prey.

Happily, golden eagle numbers are rising and rising with them are the numbers of white-tailed, or sea, eagles. One of our most successful reintroductions, they have populated the west coast of Scotland with a particularly strong presence on the Isle of Mull. This being so, it may surprise people to know that they too take mountain hares in the Cairngorms. However, these birds easily rise to a height of 1000 metres and from there, with their acute eyesight, can see the east coast.

Unlike with the eagles, the hares take little notice of buzzards and ravens, who confine their attention to the old and sick. Removing the diseased, of course, protects other hares from infection. They can hardly be expected to understand that, but a healthy adult hare will not display signs of alarm in their presence. Another reintroduced species, the red kite, a scavenger rather than a hunter, will not attack hares in any condition or at any age, but clears the roads of traffic casualties.

Among the mammals, the fox is probably the most effective predator but, like the hares, their numbers are heavily controlled by the sporting estates. Even in winter, they can be found in the higher reaches of the Northern Corries and in the Lairig Ghru. They also take ptarmigan and, in fresh snow, their pawprints are easily followed to a hare carcass or a pile of white feathers, with their droppings left nearby for further identification.

A stoat on the prowl.

Among trees and in rocky outlets, pine martens will take hares of any size. One of the most efficient of British predators, it seems to hunt not only for food but is also driven by a deep-seated instinct to kill. A marten in a hen house kills everything, as many crofters have found to their cost and to their horror.

Equally effective as a predator but carrying an air of precision in their tightly held body shape and observational manner, stoats will not usually attempt adult hares, but will take leverets. I once witnessed a stoat systematically killing, not leverets on this occasion, but eight rabbit kits as, one by one it nipped the backs of their necks, severing their spinal columns. This was one of those occasions when the photographer had a crisis of conscience, struggling not to interfere with the workings of nature. The struggle proved worth it, to watch the stoat drag the dead kits, again one by one, with great effort, through the heather to stash them as larder for itself and its young.

Among the more surprising of hare predators, for most people, are otters, which are normally thought of as hunters of fish. Some of my most successful pictures are of otters by the sea, but they also inhabit rivers, a shared habitat. Having developed a taste for hare meat they have also extended their territory in the ceaseless hunt for protein. Another of my gamekeeper friends reports how he followed a trail of otter prints from the river, across the snow, into the higher reaches of his hills, only to note the one line turning into three. It was a mother otter showing her cubs where to find mountain hares and demonstrating how to kill.

Fox.

LEFT: Red kites, another successful reintroduction, often scavenge road-killed mountain hares.

ABOVE: Otters take rabbits when they forage near the coast and will also take mountain hares when operating from inland rivers.

— *Field Note* —
Close encounter with an eagle

Lyndsey and I were out one February day when our attention was drawn to a pair of ravens in courtship display. Cameras drawn, we moved to the edge of the corrie, hoping to capture some images of their dynamic aerial display. A dark shadow on the periphery of my vision took my attention. I turned and, trying to control my excitement, whispered: 'There's a golden eagle heading our way!'

It was a female, and she passed before we could react but, to our astonishment, she turned again, and flew straight back towards us, glaring at us all the while. So close to our heads did she fly, that we could hear the air passing across her wings.

LEFT: Buzzards take mostly leverets,
but also scavenge.

ABOVE: White-tailed, or sea, eagles,
frequent visitors from the west coast,
are now breeding in the Cairngorms.

White-tailed eagle

Many years ago, I was told that true naturalists do not look for encounters. Knowing their landscape they unconsciously scan as they go. While approaching the foot of a hill in Inverness-shire I once became aware of a boulder I had passed many times, that somehow appeared to be different. Looking more closely I spotted this white-tailed eagle perched on top.

Just as it took off I managed to fire off a few camera shots. For a moment I was concerned that I had spooked the bird but, because it flew directly towards and over me, I am confident this was not the case. Its ring number was SC18.

SPRING AND SUMMER

In spring the ambient temperature on the hill can vary between -15 and +15C in only a few days. It can also be deceptive, as snow turns to sleet and rain, and warm sunny days eventually lead into the lambing snows. This is when the older hares, and the sick, tend to die, those who are not taken by predators.

Now they morph from white into the mottled brown of spring, and then to dark brown with a faint, but clearly visible, bluish hue, which is why they are sometimes referred to as 'blue hares'. They roll on the heather and scratch vigorously, replacing the deep insulating fur of winter with long, blue guard hairs that serve to protect the skin and their developing, dark brown, summer pelage. Their backs tend to become brown first as they scratch with a feline flexibility. Indeed, they have other catlike features as they are fastidiously clean and instinctively quick.

As the hill gradually warms, activity levels rise for both sexes. The heather softens, grasses grow greener and their diet improves. This is essential, especially for the jills whose rich milk will grow their tiny offspring by as much as thirty grams per day. The first litters start to appear in early April and some jills might have three, or even four in a season, each of three or four leverets.

Of course, they are not the only creatures to breed at this time. Black grouse gather at the leks (Swedish for a 'gathering place'), the males strutting back and forward with sexual intensity. Red grouse are hatching on the moors. Dotterel have returned to share the higher ground with the ptarmigan, who never left. Dippers are searching the hill streams for insects while golden plover move up from the flood plain. Golden eagles have rapidly growing chicks to feed. I describe the ring ouzel as the 'vicar of blackbirds' to my clients, as that is

The mountain hare as philosopher.

how it looks with its striking, white collar. I also tell them they are never alone on the hill, that many pairs of eyes will always be watching.

Parenting is a matter of indifference for male hares, who remain by the females only to be ready when they come back into season. It is a brief enough exercise for the females, who leave their offspring to their own devices as quickly as possible to produce another litter.

The hares, who show signs of deep concern in the presence of buzzards and ravens, are petrified when the shadow of an eagle glides across the hill. They physically cower, their eyes widening with alarm. Although their best defence is stillness and the natural camouflage their pelage provides, they become indecisive with heightening fear. To run or not?

Unlike other grazing animals, who tend to move across the gradient, along the contours, hares usually flee up or down. If they flee upwards they generally survive, as the eagle finds it difficult to swoop against the rising slope. Downwards, and they generally die when struck by the eagle's talons, or later in its crushing, piercing grip. So much for the adults, but the leverets are more of a sitting resource, to be taken in high numbers not only by eagles but also wildcats,

A young hare enjoying the sun.

ravens, buzzards, pine martens and, in single bites, foxes. Survival for the species depends not on deep nurturing but on many births, and many losses.

Within this welter of change, spring turns to summer and the heat increases, especially close to the ground. The hares respond by moving higher but, even there, can be seen panting to stay cool. With the breeding season now past, and the invoice paid in flesh for their frantic mating and birthing, their task is to put on weight and improve their condition against the next change in season. They can be quite particular in what they eat, and individual hares seem to have their favourite foods.

I have watched a hare sniffing and tasting for the best single blade of grass in a clump.

In spring and summer, the challenges for the photographer lie in the management of light. In the earlier conditions, the sun's rays tend to dazzle. Later, especially when photographing from a prone position, heat haze and shimmer can distort the image. It is a sort of privilege though, to catch them against what remains of the snow, or to picture their fresh brown coats on moors that soon, in autumn, will blossom in purple. It can feel as if the mountain hare is not just one species but three or four, and the fascination of their individuality is endless.

Never completely still for long.

LEFT: Plenty of winter coat still on.

ABOVE: A private place.

LEFT: The perfect insulation when dry.

ABOVE: Dodging the lambing snow.

The Boxers

With Richard, a cameraman from BBC's *The One Show*, I had been commissioned to film mountain hares boxing in the snow. This winter had been so unpredictable though, the snow could be gone in a few days. Richard called from London to ask about conditions. There was hardly any snow on higher ground, but a blast of cold air was due from the Arctic. The decision was made to proceed with all fingers and toes well and truly crossed and, on a clear and bright morning, we rode an Argo-cat loaded with gear up the hillside, clinging on for dear life. It was 'game-on'!

The only way to get good footage of mountain hares boxing is to get yourself into the thick of the action among a decently sized population. I knew just the place and it proved to hold no fewer than twenty-five. Climbing on foot to just below them we set up the gear and waited… and waited… until…

… until a jack came charging across the hill, straight for a hare we knew for certain was a jill. This was the moment we were waiting for. He slowed to make his approach, gingerly easing towards her, sniffing the air as he moved closer. In the blink of an eye, she spun around and knocked seven bells out of him. A chase ensued. They dashed back and forward in ever tightening circles until, face-to-face, they reared up and boxed. As quickly as it had started, it stopped, and the jack ran off in the direction he'd come.

I turned to ask Richard if he had caught the action, but his wide grin said it all.

SPRING AND SUMMER COMPANIONS

ABOVE: Ptarmigan almost into summer plumage.

RIGHT: Black grouse cocks in mid-battle.

ABOVE: The classic pose...

RIGHT: ...followed by a more casual look.

Field Note

Hare shaking the rain
off its pelage

Inspiration came while watching a hare shaking rain off its pelage; but planning and capturing these pictures took another five months. The idea was never far from my mind until, one day, I awoke to a forecast of heavy rain with intermittent sunny intervals, the two elements I would need. All I had to do was find a hare with the sun behind it, to give just a hint of backlight.

That day, it was my great good fortune to locate a relaxed and sleepy hare in a slightly elevated position, almost at eye level as I lay on the ground. A heavy rainfall followed and, oh boy, did it rain. For two hours it came down in stair-rods. We were both soaked through. Another half hour went past before the hare's nose started to twitch, and its mouth moved from side to side: sure signs of coming activity… and then it happened!

The hare stood up and shook, raindrops flew in every direction and filled the frame with droplets of water, exactly as I'd envisaged five months before. Nor did it stop there. He proceeded to lick and clean his ears, paws and pelage for another twenty minutes, presenting me with some unique and, at times, amusing poses.

All good things come to those who wait.

SPRING AND SUMMER COMPANIONS

LEFT: Dipper with salmon parr.

ABOVE: Male ring ouzel.

ABOVE: Scratch...

RIGHT: ...and wash.

Haring down the road

Visit the hares for a few years and you get to know how they behave. While photographing grouse I spotted this hare running along the road nearby. It would surely return, and a front shot would be more exciting than a shot of the animal's rear end.

Risking life and limb I lay on the road and waited, thinking it might take ten minutes. In fact, it took forty! A friendly driver stopped to ask if I was alright, perplexed by the mad photographer apparently taking pictures of the road surface.

LEFT: Ready...
ABOVE: ...and go.

SPRING AND SUMMER COMPANIONS

Left: Dotterel.

Above: Golden plover.

ABOVE: A curious look...

RIGHT: ...and a sideways glance.

LEVERETS

The first litters of the year are born between the middle and end of April: brown, fully furred and with their eyes wide open. From the outset they can flee predators, but not speedily. Not being agile on their tiny legs they are more likely to tunnel into the heather. Immensely appealing, a leveret will fit comfortably into the hollow of a normal human hand, but I ask my clients to resist the temptation on ethical grounds. Good practice means 'observation without interference'.

It is not that the jill will reject her offspring, although her mothering has the appearance of abandonment. This near abandonment being part of nature's strategy, she will tuck her litter into a peat bank or heather patch, out of harm's way, while she seeks the sustenance required to produce a milk rich enough to grow them with incredible rapidity. Very quickly, the leverets extend their territory, making distance one from another, and from this widening circle she draws them in, twice daily, to suckle. From about Day 15 they will be on a mixed diet of milk and grazing.

The survival instinct in the new generation is sharp from the outset. They are under immediate and constant danger from predators and there is no strength in numbers, rather the opposite. Better to be scattered as widely as practical. They will not stray far from each other by human standards, but the distance is significant to the character of the individual and the nature of the community. As they become stronger, they range more widely and the bonds between littermates and mother, never tight in human terms, loosen and part.

The jill gives birth between one and three times a season and her young must be fully independent when the next litter comes along, typically, two months later. It all fits.

The leverets have tiny ears with a white tuft at the top of their heads, and pale irises that darken with maturity.

New born.

65

They are imbued with explosive energy and can dash like an electric fluffball, five or ten metres, from beneath a walker's feet to the safety of a boulder. Or the walker might half notice a line of movement under the heather and wonder if this is a hallucination.

My preference is to wait motionlessly at a likely location, and I like to talk quietly and steadily until they are used to the unthreatening sound of my voice. Often, I will stop with my clients and ask them what they hear: the sound of the river, the wind as it rounds the hillside, perhaps the distant thunder of warplanes practicing at altitude. This is their customary aural background and, as stalkers of a kind, we should join it if we can. Before too many minutes we will be taken as a normal presence.

Against this, they do not like sudden or surprising noises such as shouting or the sound of zips and Velcro.

Eventually, a little pair of ears will appear above a boulder and out they will come to rehearse all the stretching and yawning, a paw stretching high five (high four?), scratching and nibbling rituals that the adults go through, but with an additional level of miniature appeal. Over the years I have given names to a few I have known from their early lives: Bagpuss, Mrs G, Rita, necessary identifications but also favourite hares with appealing characters and recognisable mannerisms.

The minority of leverets who survive the predations of stoats, buzzards, ravens, wind and rain, enter

Leveret hiding in purple heather.

the autumn period and their first moult at about three quarters of their adult size. Many would be indistinguishable from smaller adults but for their youthful faces. Most people term these hares 'yearlings', meaning they are within their first year of life. They are ready for the ordeal of their first winter. Survive that, and they will breed the following spring. The great cycle of life will continue.

It is all too easy to assign human qualities to the mountain hare. Their frequent representation in our mythologies and art points, or seems to point, towards human connection. So too does the quickness of their eyes, how they will sometimes search the landscape from an upright position and, of course,

the boxing matches. Too much can be made of this anthropomorphism, or so I tell my clients, but the 'observation without interference' rule can be difficult to maintain while the leverets are taken by a predator or freezing in the rain. Nature must be left to get on with it, I say, and death is nothing more than a natural part of living.

What though, one of my clients asked, if the hare is one of your special, named ones? Since there is no real connection, and no significance to the name but the identification of a specimen, can you watch with equanimity? The answer to that is in the deep silence behind the wind and the river's noise, in the environment we share.

LEFT: Perfect camouflage, or a study in browns.

ABOVE: Enjoying the view.

LEFT: Morning has broken.

ABOVE: First stretch of the day.

The Leveret

A friend and I were resting while looking for Ptarmigan in the high Cairngorms when a sudden movement caught his eye. He nudged me and looked at a large boulder no more than twenty metres from where we sat with breath held.

After a few minutes, the cutest wee face of a very young leveret appeared. Soon, it gained enough confidence to leave the sanctuary of its boulder. I lost count how many photographs I took of this endearing little creature as it preened and cleaned itself, just as an adult hare would.

Objective photographer as I am, I eventually found myself sitting back to just watch its antics, enchanted by the charm of this young hare.

LEFT: Learning about this strange new world...

ABOVE: ...and starting to explore.

LEFT: Time out to relax.

ABOVE: Time out for thought.

Give me a high four!

Very rarely do you come across a hare as laid back as this one. We spent many hours together, during which it would sleep for a while and then wake up to entertain me with its antics. Its form was a little cup in the mossy surface of the moor, so positioned that I could shoot eye to eye. This allowed me to capture these highly intimate images of the animal saluting, yawning, stretching and delivering a celebratory high four.

At home in the form.

ABOVE: Ever alert.

RIGHT: Who goes there?

AUTUMN

The smells and sounds of autumn tend to run a poor second to the visual power of the grouse moors. Awash with purple in this season, they have become so much a cliché of romantic Scotland that the reality of their being a managed environment is too easily forgotten. The smells and sounds though, are vivid. To be alive on the high moors is to be contained within a bubble of sweetness. It is to be assailed with the sounds of bees, active among the blossom, to be in the company of dragonflies and moths, red deer and mountain hares whose youngest are, by now, about half their final size.

There will be no more litters this year. This being so, the mature hares are free to escape the increasing irritation of mites and tics by migrating uphill. The move is significant and, for some, will be fatal as many estate owners contend that the tics they carry host a virus that attacks the grouse. Conservationists, in turn, point out that there is no science to support the notion of reduced grouse numbers for this reason. The debate continues, but across too many estates hares are culled in their tens of thousands.

My own view is that the mountain hare is not uniquely culpable for the migration of tics and is used, in fact, as a sort of fall guy. Other animals, including game animals, must be held to be equally responsible.

I have photographed hares while a grouse shoot has been in progress nearby. The shooters roar up in 4x4s and take their places in shooting butts that are constructed along the slope at regular intervals. Stationed at their elbows, the ghillies' facility in breaking, emptying and reloading is imperative to the steady continuity of the killing. Teams of beaters advance through the heather, shouting and waving flags to raise the birds explosively from under their feet, that they might fly over the waiting guns and be blown out of the sky one by one. Guns are exchanged,

Mountain hare and grass changing colour together.

the dogs race to retrieve the dead birds, another volley is fired. The barrels are warm, even hot; the smell of cordite lingers. Empty cartridges litter the ground. The hares and I go about our simple, quiet business as best we can.

The shooting parties are highly, even delightfully, choreographed and are the crescendo of the Estate year. Beginning on the 'Glorious' 12th August, they continue until the 10th December, or thereabouts, and represent the principal, annual payoff for the year's work. Out of season, the law is frequently broken by shooting at impermissible times, and the illegal persecution of raptors and other predators such as hen harriers, which are referred to as 'vermin'. Over-zealousness on the more heavily managed estates promotes a monoculture that amounts to the eradication of all life that is not grouse. In the modern era, much of this is captured on video by hillwalkers and photographers and posted online. Some raptors these days are tagged and monitored by satellite. To say that a reckoning is coming is an observation, not wishful thinking.

More elevating images in this season are plentiful. The eaglets have fledged but still return to the nest with their parents, learning the craft of being eagles. We watch them circling the hill, easily discerning the

Taking off.

young by the strong white patterns on the underside of their wings. Dotterel, having hatched their one or two broods, leave early for North Africa. Golden plovers depart the high ground. The salmon come back to spawn, and ospreys follow the line of the river before returning to their large, messy nests in Strathspey. Stags are roaring on the hill, the authentic voice of Scottish wildness. Such is the intensity of their competition for hinds that I have seen some dead after a charge that has dug their antlers into the ground and broken their necks.

The days shorten, the temperature drops, and the mountain hares' coats begin their return to white in mid to late October. It tends to start with a rim around the eye, followed by the collar and the neck and then the whole coat. Since it is a process triggered by hormones, and hares are individuals, not all turn at the same time, and it is far from unusual to observe one that is fully white sitting beside one that is still completely brown.

As the season advances, grasses turn from green to gold, the hill effects a different palette and it is a beautiful experience to photograph the mountain hares against the background of these new colours. Soon there will be snow, but now… the shutter closes, and the picture is taken.

Early autumn sequence.

ABOVE: Happy in heather.

RIGHT: Room with a view.

Field Note

A hare for all seasons

One of my quests has been to photograph mountain hares through the seasons, capturing every aspect of their mysterious lives in all conditions. This being so I planned the series of images shown here months in advance. It was a matter of finding the right hare on a favourable day. By great good luck, one solitary hare proved to have a confiding nature and was quite a performer, displaying this series of behavioural gestures every twenty minutes or so.

AUTUMN COMPANIONS

LEFT: Red grouse in flight.

ABOVE: Juvenile dotterel preparing to
leave for Africa.

Field Note
Pretty in purple

One September day in Inverness-shire, when the air was thick with midges, I paid a visit to a young hare I had developed an affection for. Knowing that it would soon move for more food, I waited with my camera. When it did, I stealthily followed, losing it behind a bank of heather in bloom but understanding that this was an opportunity to win a low perspective image.

During my final approach I had noticed that whenever my jacket rustled its head would pop up and it would look at me quizzically. Positioning myself carefully I rustled my jacket again, and this perfect image was the result.

AUTUMN COMPANIONS

LEFT: Migrating salmon.

ABOVE: Osprey with trout.

The yawning hare

Much as I cherish every moment spent with mountain hares, I admit that their lengthy sleeping time tests my patience to the limit. Saying that though, I've learned that patience is usually rewarded.

Among the first indications that a hare is about to wake are a twitching of the nose followed by the bottom jaw moving from side to side. Almost immediately afterwards it will bend to collect a pellet from its anus and eat it with a rapturous licking of the lips. What follows depends on the individual, but usually involves a big yawn and stretch.

I've lost count of how often I've photographed this behaviour, but it makes me smile every time.

LEFT: Ears back – Caution!

ABOVE: Something on my nose.

Field Note

The morphing hare

The problem with 'snapshots in time' is that, by definition, they cannot demonstrate change. I managed to photograph this hare in the same form, in the same posture, in the Monadhliath hills, four times over twenty-eight days – in not quite equal periods. The resultant sequence shows it morphing into its winter pelage in what really is an amazing and beautiful process. My admiration and affection for this hare was sadly one sided, as you can tell from its expression.

AUTUMN COMPANIONS

LEFT: The season takes it toll. A spent salmon.

ABOVE: The ultimate symbol of
Highland Scotland.

ABOVE: Listening for people noises.

RIGHT: Who could not love them?

WINTER

This is my favourite time for photographing hares, but it presents tremendous challenges. In the high Cairngorms temperatures can plummet to -15C. Add wind chill and the effective temperature can drop as low as -30. The Northern Corries offer some shelter but allow for spindrift and drifting snow, and conditions are correctly termed 'Arctic'. The photographer at least gets to go home at night.

There are also advantages. For one thing, the period of low angled light that we term the golden hour can extend for four hours, during which the colours and details of the hares' coats and the surrounding landscape are enhanced. For another, they don't move about all that much. Instead, they sit with their backs to the wind as a horseshoe of snow builds around them and, thanks to the area of low pressure in front, mounds under their noses. Drifting in and out of slumber, they occasionally lean against the wall of the

form thus created before shaking themselves awake again.

For additional protection, they will occasionally turn and dig in, eventually creating a tunnel as layers of snow build. They are literally living on the edge of survival with only ptarmigan still accompanying them after 10,000 years.

When food becomes too scarce they will climb to the edge of the plateau where the snow is scoured thin by the wind, to dig through the ice with their tough little claws in search of dead vegetation. Nothing can be wasted so, since they cannot easily digest cellulose, they host bacteria in their gut that breaks the substance down and eat of it a second time as pellets snatched from the anus. In the absence of standing, unfrozen water they will eat snow. The living is meagre, but they must ingest energy for their coats to perform their vital double function: keeping

Curling up for the night.

out the wind while retaining the heat generated in their bodies.

On the rocky edges they sit in the lee of boulders and look over Strathspey almost like resting mountaineers but, no doubt, with an eye for the eagles. Easy prey when seen, they are protected by their natural camouflage which may be pure white, or close to graphite grey with all variations between, and is incredibly silken and dense to the touch. Their ears, when laid flat, leave an indentation that I find to be charming, and are made visible by their black tips like eyes in the backs of their heads.

I have never seen an iced-up mountain hare, but to achieve this takes maintenance. Stepping out of their forms, every half hour or so, they will engage in some of their most delightful behaviour: the high five stretch, the face rub, the pellet grab, rolling in the snow to clean their pelage, and they do a lot of yawning. Movement can't be wasted. The fluffiness game is a matter of life and death.

Sometimes they will run, splaying their toes wide to act as snowshoes as they float across the snow although, if their camouflage has been seen through, it is probably too late. My fear is that it is not the eagles that are their most implacable predator, nor the wildcats, buzzards and foxes. Global warming has already created change. On my other main stomping ground, the Monadhliath hills, there is no off-season for tics, which now survive on high ground all year round, and there are fewer hares than in living memory. My friend Lewis, a gamekeeper on one of the more enlightened estates, says his hilltop 'used to heave, it was like a blizzard of hares'.

Downhill and downwind, the jack has an enquiring sniff.

These 'slightly warmer' conditions present the most lethal danger. When an animal's fur is soaked and flattened it can no longer do the job it evolved to do. Air cannot be trapped within it, nor retain heat. The hare's energy is sucked out and, as previously noted, replenishment is scarce. Climate change is the great existential threat to the mountain hare. Greater than its predators which, when left in peace, will maintain a balance. Greater than the shooting estates and their overzealous culls which will soon, hopefully, be consigned to the past. Their essential, seasonal, dry cold is departing and leaving them vulnerable to wind driven rain.

Still though, conditions remain good for the species. Hard enough to kill off the weak and the old. Survivable enough for the young and strong. I spend as much as four hours with a single hare, alone or with clients from many countries: Germany, Scandinavia, Canada, the Middle East, all points of the compass, who boost the Highland economy.

As we move towards spring the hares' year begins another hormonal round and the boxing starts again. I watch them with unqualified admiration for the ways they endure and for how long. While they sleep their mouths slide from side to side, their ears twitch and their eyes move behind their lids. Like us, they dream… but of what? Longer days and richer grasses? I like to think that, from the deep wells of species memory, there might arise images of ice sheets and glaciers, of polar bears, musk ox and bison, the arrival of the first humans.

Left: Shaking off some snow.

Above: Visiting the snack bar.

LEFT: Mountain hare wise....

ABOVE: ...and mountain hare wary.

ABOVE: Back to the wind in the Northern Corries.

LEFT: Storm over, what's doing?

LEFT: Playing it cool.

ABOVE: Scraping for food.

Field Note

Creating an icon

While seeking ptarmigan high in the Cairngorms I found myself distracted by dozens of hares on the corrie floor. One took my eye and I made a slow approach by, first, tobogganing down the slope on my belly, camera and tripod held above my head. In the course of my hour-long crawl a blizzard came in and covered both hares and photographer.

When I finally settled and waited, the hare did what I could barely have hoped for by moving round its boulder, no doubt for improved shelter, and looking me straight in the eye.

This was one of my most productive sessions and gave the front jacket image for this book, an image that put my career on an upward trajectory.

ABOVE: Glancing over her shoulder....

RIGHT: ...and saying hello to the world.

LEFT: I'm so tired...

ABOVE: ...but always ready to run.

ABOVE: Heavy weather coming in.

RIGHT: Shelter from the storm.

Field Note

Winter habitat

Over a metre of snow had fallen overnight and the clouds were still dark and lowering. The walk up the mountain was, to say the least, laborious, but near the top was a familiar location which was home to at least two dozen mountain hares. None were to be seen though.

Casting around widely, I eventually spotted a newly dug mound of snow and realised they were tucked into deep tunnels they had been excavating continually during the storm, which explained why they were so difficult to find. Only the tips of their noses were visible.

Over the next half hour, I built a little wall of snow to not only keep me relatively snug against the elements, but also to serve as a makeshift hide. Another half hour and they were happily moving around with no suspicion of me or my camera.

The images captured over the wall perfectly represent what a mountain hare endures on a brutally cold winter's day.

LEFT: Patiently waiting for spring.

ABOVE: Sitting pretty.

ABOVE: Dusted with fresh fallen snow.

RIGHT: Instinctively running uphill.

ABOVE: The hare looks at the camera.

RIGHT: Mirror image.

Green eyed hare

Spend as much time as I do with a single species and you will notice subtle differences between individuals. For example, some hares have ears that are long and thin, where others are short and thick. Some have square tips, others large black tips. Another point of difference is the colour of their whiskers, which can be either black or white.

The one physical feature that captures the hearts of most people is their deep alluring eyes. They certainly capture mine. Mostly they are deep orange, although in younger hares and leverets they are more of a pale gold.

This image is unique in my collection as the hare clearly has a green iris, the first and only time I've noticed this.

THE FAMOUS MATING RITUAL
KNOWN AS BOXING

ABOVE: Showing an interest.

RIGHT: Too far, too fast.

THE FAMOUS MATING RITUAL
KNOWN AS BOXING

LEFT: The sheer athleticism of boxing hares....

ABOVE: ...is as close to dance as conflict.

THE FAMOUS MATING RITUAL
KNOWN AS BOXING

ABOVE: The contest can go on for quite a while...

RIGHT: ...but arrives at its natural conclusion

Three in a row

Mountain hares are mostly solitary, but conditions will sometimes send them into close proximity on the narrow leeward side of certain hills. Two hares took the attention of my only client of the day and me but were not sufficiently interesting for us to abandon the subject in front of us. Until, that is, a third joined them at such a spacing as to create this perfect pattern. We abandoned our immediate project and relocated with our cameras and tripods. In the right place at the right time when chance delivered opportunity, and we could not let it go past.

LEFT: Enjoying a pelage-cleaning snow bath.
ABOVE: Followed by a snooze.

ABOVE: Running on frozen snow.

RIGHT: Winter companion. Ptarmigan.

ABOVE: Approaching winter's end.

RIGHT: Backlit in the afternoon.

LEFT: Shining like a beacon at sundown.

ABOVE: Last light of the day.

THREE OF A KIND

To achieve a deep understanding of any species takes time and patience and my love affair with mountain hares has developed over a long period. Little did I know, when I began, that this affection would deepen as it did and ultimately alter the course of my life. My emotional connection with the animals is a frequent source of surprise to me, but I am not alone in this. Some of my clients have complained of the difficulty of focusing their cameras when their eyes are filled with tears.

Like people, like my clients, the hares have individual characteristics: some are shy and retiring, others more sociable, even brazen. After many hours in their company I have come to really know a few 'very special' hares and, in this chapter, I'll introduce you to three.

Stretching a paw.

153

Rita

I first met Rita when she was a young leveret of about three months, living on a working grouse moor. Almost nonchalant towards me from the first encounter, it was apparent that she was 'different'. So charmed was I that I took Lyndsey to see her and we sat watching while she dozed in the sun. When she woke, she stretched, strolled up to Lyndsey, and casually sniffed her knee before hopping away to graze on heather and grasses. Lyndsey's face was the picture.

So strong were my feelings for Rita that I asked the estate's head keeper if he would put a hunting exclusion around her normal territory so that she would not be culled with the others. Such was his empathy not only with me, but with the hares he was obliged to kill, that he agreed. Her survival led to many encounters that were so powerful they are etched in my memory forever.

Rita is the hare I pictured between the horizon and the clouds one September, as you will see in this chapter. A month later, I suggested to a client that we pay her a visit. She didn't take long to locate. Now in her winter pelage for the first time, she posed (as she always would) in the best possible positions, giving us ample opportunities to capture images of her against the distant hillsides. We stayed long into the evening light and left her exactly where we had found her hours earlier.

ABOVE: Rita on high alert.

RIGHT: Rita, such a beautiful hare.

Bagpuss

This wonderful animal had a stripy face and always looked a bit miffed but was extremely popular among photographers of mountain hares. It was his confiding and trusting nature that made him so approachable. I could hardly believe my eyes in the Natural History Museum, in London, when I found his picture on everything from placemats to keyrings. He even made it onto the front cover of Black and White photography magazine, and became the first ever 'celebrity' hare? We had many memorable encounters.

It was he who taught me to read and understand the body language of the mountain hare. I would find him in late November or early December in the same form and under the same boulder, from which he would range for only a few hundred metres. Bagpuss was very much a ladies' man. If there was a jill coming into season you could be certain that Bagpuss would be interested. The last time I saw him he chased two jills around the hillside, mating first with one and then the other.

Bagpuss, cute as ever.

Mrs G

The winter pelage and facial features of one of my subjects, Mrs G, in many respects resembled those of Bagpuss, and she behaved in a very similar manner. I often wonder if she was part of his legacy. Her name derives from her winter colour, which is quite unusually dark grey. She lived on a high windy plateau and, in the two years I knew her, only ever wandered a few hundred metres from her form.

In spring 2017, I photographed her sitting on a patch of snow. Beneath her, unbeknown to me, was a small hole containing one of her leverets. The delightful little animal popped its head out and looked in our direction. Fearlessly, it walked up to her and nuzzled at her belly. This was the holy grail of mountain hare photography: a leveret suckling, which usually happens under cover of darkness. Sadly, she swiped her offspring away before I could take the picture. Hopefully, one day...

What makes these hares so confident in human company baffles me. Perhaps it is something in their genetic make-up? High in the Cairngorms I frequently encounter hares that are happy to be photographed, in an area with no culling. Possibly they are influenced by the high instance of human presence in recreational areas such as the Cairngorm and Monadhliath hills? Or is it quite simply down to the character of the individual hare?

If it were not for these three 'very special' individuals (and some others), it would have been much more difficult to learn and understand the

Mrs G portrait.

language of the mountain hare. To get close to one is always energising, but to gain its trust and revisit time and time again is a privilege. It allows me, as a wildlife photographer, to achieve the deep understanding that I seek.

Sunset Hare

It's not often a photographic session runs entirely to plan. Many things can work for or against you. Almost on a whim, I paid a visit to Rita, who lived on open moorland twenty minutes from my home near Inverness. Dozing in the afternoon sun, she turned and glanced in my direction with anxious eyes. I talked softly to her, and almost immediately she settled.

I knew this hare well, having first photographed her as a leveret and later keeping track of her as she grew into a beautiful sub-adult. From previous experience, with her and others, I knew that late in the day they sometimes leave the relative safety of their forms. Positioning myself carefully, I noticed a break between the clouds and the distant mountains and thought that this could be rather spectacular.

Everything came together like magic. Just as she began to graze, the setting sun touched the horizon, washing the moor with evening light. The hare's pelage was surrounded by a halo of gold.

LEFT AND ABOVE: Rita in Autumn.

LEFT: Rita taking a nap.

ABOVE: Rita's pelage changes from blue to white in preparation for winter.

LEFT: Rita grazing contentedly.

ABOVE: Rita plays hard to get.

Field Note

Bagpuss, gourmet of grass

Bagpuss had a penchant for the grass-like heath rush *Juncus squarrosus*. He would not only haunt the areas where it grew but also carefully select individual stems. No reckless glutton he but, as I liked to think of him, a gourmet of grass. Of the hares I have known only he was sufficiently trusting to allow me to take such close and intimate images. These moments I shared with Bagpuss will live with me forever.

ABOVE: Bagpuss enjoying a scratch.

RIGHT: Bagpuss stoic as the snow falls.

ABOVE: Bagpuss makes his feelings known.

RIGHT: Bagpuss, an intimate portrait.

LEFT: Bagpuss sticks out his tongue.

ABOVE: Bagpuss enjoys a mega-yawn.

LEFT: Bagpuss, low perspective.

ABOVE: Bagpuss shakes off the rain.

Bagpuss steals the show

Bagpuss was the perfect candidate for a hare I could photograph through every month of the year, and I managed to capture wonderful images in the months from November through to July. However, in July of each year I repeatedly lost him as his intensity in seeking out jills in season took him to places beyond my knowing. This sequence was taken just before I lost him *again*, but what a show he put on.

ABOVE: Bagpuss when grazing is scarce.

RIGHT: Bagpuss takes a bow.

Field Note

Blowing in the wind with Mrs G

Mrs G was being obliging, as usual, perched in one of her favourite locations. Her summer coat was coming through, so she was preening herself more than she would at other times of the year. I noticed that tiny bits of fluff that she dislodged were floating off in the wind. There's a challenge for a photographer! As the clouds were also being blown past it became part of the challenge to frame the dislodged white tuft on a blue background framed by the white clouds and ground surface.

ABOVE: Mrs G cleaning her back.

RIGHT: Mrs G attends to her ears.

LEFT: Mrs G does a pellet grab.

ABOVE: Mrs G washes her face.

LEFT: Mrs G splays her toes before
fully stretching her leg.

ABOVE: Mrs G adopts a pose.

189

ABOVE: A reverse portrait of Mrs G.

RIGHT: Mrs G runs to meet me,
as she often did.

CREDO
THE MOUNTAIN HARE
AND THE CAMERA

Over the years I have introduced hundreds of people to the charms of the mountain hare, and many have fallen head over heels in love. From first noticing this emotional, or 'connecting', response I have felt enormously privileged in the role of facilitator. The act of photographing them for me, which I now understand is true for most people, is enormously satisfying. It is not too much to say that the hares have changed my life: not only in terms of employment but also in relation to my approach to other people. They encourage a sort of openness, a generosity of being, and I am more than happy to pass on what I have learned about photographing them.

The approach is probably the single most critical thing. Do it badly and you'll spook every hare you find. They get nervous when approached from opposite directions. If you are on the hill with friends, stay together and approach in a direct but very slow manner. If the hare isn't comfortable it will start to twitch, warming its muscles in readiness for flight, and lie flat with its ears pressed firmly onto its back. If it looks away from you, it's checking that it has somewhere to run, probably uphill.

You should walk slowly and directly forwards. The hare will be happier with you clearly in sight. When you are within a hundred metres, check its posture. Is it still where you first spotted it? If so, proceed. If it's looking nervous, sit down. It may take anything up to fifteen minutes to settle again. Patience in the photographer is of the essence. Patience in the hare is variable, but its end is sharply delineated.

When you get within fifty metres drop to the ground and crawl slowly forwards. I cannot emphasise enough the importance of slowness. If the hare continues to twitch and move around: stop. Wait for it to settle before restarting your crawl. Your speed of approach will be determined by the tolerance of that individual

The mountain hare and the photographer.

Patience rewarded.

hare, but don't push your luck. Each hare has a 'circle of fear' which can only be judged with experience. Hares that will accept you within a few metres are rare. 'Quiet' fabric outer garments really help, so avoid materials that rustle.

It's not unusual to spend five or even six hours with a hare. If you're lucky it will preen and clean itself or stretch and yawn. Take your time and drink deep of the experience. Treat the hares with respect and they will reward you with an insight into their mysterious world.

***

Photography is an art form and there is no right or wrong way to do it, but the following few points may be borne in mind.

A low perspective gives an image a more intimate feel, so, if possible try to position yourself lower than your subject. Hares often cooperate, albeit unconsciously, by sitting on small ledges on the hillside.

Although hares photograph well from almost every angle, side-on looks great; especially on a steep sided slope. Face on works best at a low angle if, given time and a careful approach by the photographer, the hare remains tolerant of the intrusion.

As in all photography light is the most important factor and using it to best effect is a skill that comes with experience. Therefore, the more time spent outside with the hares the better. Front-light, sometimes referred to as over-the-shoulder light, is commonly used, but is not as straightforward as you might think, especially when the hares are in their white pelage. Light meters can be confused by white subjects and, with a white hare on snow, a camera may automatically darken the image. To compensate we must adjust the exposure by as much as two to three stops. Similarly, with a white hare against a dark background we reverse the process and underexpose by anything up to two stops.

Some species photograph back-lit really well, and mountain hares are one, but it helps that they have a distinctive, easily recognised profile. If the sun is low, a back-lit image should be possible. Keep your eye open for a glow radiating from its fur, and choose an angle which offers a clean background, preferably in shadow. Underexpose by as much as four or five full stops to ensure only the brightest of the highlights are captured. With luck and skill, the hare will be radiant.

Shooting wider while keeping the hare small in the frame displays the animal in its environment and locates it in the narrative of hare and habitat.

Portraits are the most popular style of photography, and mountain hares are the perfect subjects, but remember to hang back and give them space. They are decently small at rest but, when they stand up and stretch, can triple in height and length. Don't forget to increase your depth-of-field when shooting close up, and always focus on the hare's eye.

A word of warning is appropriate here: get too close and there is a risk the hare will flee or worse. A fellow photographer once told me of a hare that hissed at her. I hadn't heard of this before and enquired further to learn that she had attempted an image using a wide-angle lens at very close quarters, which stressed the hare into reacting. Such practices are unacceptable as an animal should never fear for its life. The welfare of the hare is paramount.

For me, by now, time spent with hares has transcended photography to become an engulfing passion. My desire to know more of their mysterious lives only grows stronger, and every encounter I have is etched into my memory. Looking at any of the images in my vast archive I am instantly transported back to the location, and recall the sights, sounds and smells of the day. I do not think of myself as a deeply spiritual person, but these encounters do spiritually move me.

In my opinion the long-term prospects for the species are good. Their persecution by a few misguided humans is unfortunate but I am hopeful that protective legislation and licensing will not only be sufficient but will also be introduced before their position becomes critical. Mountain hares have been here for ten thousand years and it is my sincere hope that they will be here for many more.

If you haven't seen one at close quarters I implore you to seek them out. Their striking appearance and characterful antics are sure to endear them to you as they have to me. Strive to enjoy every part of an encounter, savouring every second of their company. Always observe; always learn. Only then will you enter the secret life of the mountain hare.

Appendix
Safety and Comfort

Remember that your own safety is paramount and is your own responsibility. Scottish mountains take lives every year. There are many books of guidance on the subject and I would recommend *Mountaincraft and Leadership* by Eric Langmuir. There are also courses run by the National Outdoor Training Centre at Glenmore Lodge. These are recommended. For the hard end of what can happen, and by way of warning, I recommend *Cairngorm John: a life in mountain rescue* by retired leader of Cairngorm Mountain Rescue Team John Allen. The few tips offered below should act as reminders.

- Scottish mountains can be hostile places where wind chill, frostbite, and exposure are very real dangers.

- Before setting out, always check the weather forecast and be sure someone knows where you are going.

- Carry adequate food and liquids for any eventuality, as well as a fully charged mobile phone. Remember there are black-spots.

- I recommend the carrying of a storm shelter and first aid-kit.

- Adequate hillwalking clothes should be worn or carried including: warm hat, gloves, thermal layers, waterproofs, boots and, when necessary, micro-crampons. I am a brand partner with Keela, the outdoor clothes manufacturer located in Glenrothes, and test all their products to destruction – which can take quite a while, I can tell you!

- Unlike when hillwalking for hillwalking's sake, the photographer is likely to carry equipment that is both cumbersome and heavy. Avoid perspiring too much on the way up as conditions are likely to be cold over what might be hours of sitting.

Demands on some kinds of equipment can be greater than for most hillwalking.

- Binoculars: The first and most important part of photographing wildlife is to find it. I couldn't function as a professional photographer and guide without a good pair of binoculars. I've always used Leica because of their exceptional optics and supreme build quality and am a Leica ambassador. Therefore, I promote the brand with gusto and enthusiasm, which is easy to do when you believe in a product.

- Camera: I use Canon DSLR's, mainly a Canon 1DX Mk2 plus a 7D Mk2. More important than the camera body are the lenses. Not everyone can afford a large prime lens pricing at five figures, but there are lots of long reach lenses of reasonable quality at more affordable prices. The second-hand market is always worth consideration. A more powerful lens allows you to operate from further away and therefore be less intrusive.

- Tripod/beanbag: A good sturdy tripod keeps the camera stable and reduces movement. This is important when photographing more nervous hares. Bean bags can be found on-line very cheaply. Filled with rice or split-peas, they are great for working at low-levels or in areas with lots of rocks.

- Rain/weather protection cover to protect your camera equipment. Cameras and water don't mix very well.

- Spare batteries / memory cards: On cold days keep them in your inside jacket pockets as low temperatures deplete their power. When purchasing memory cards, never buy cheap. The more expensive ones write/send the data from the camera to the card at a higher speed, allowing you to take more images before the process starts to buffer. There is nothing worse than a camera buffering just as hare does something after two hours of patient waiting.

- Camping mat: I use this small but useful piece of kit for a dual purpose. By lining my backpack it helps protect my camera and lenses whilst in transit. Secondly, I can sit or lie on it, which is especially helpful on snow, or damp ground.

Cleaning off the snow.